Orthodoxy for Children

Vladimir Luchaninov

The Clergy

**Illustrations by
Vera Marova**

Grand Rapids · Exaltation Press · 2019

Copyright © 2019 Exaltation Press

Author: Vladimir Luchaninov
Illustrator: Vera Marova
Translator: Fr. John Hogg

"The Clergy"
     Starting with the Old Testament and the world before the coming of Christ, this book explains for children what a temple is and what priests are. Then, it moves on to explain the New Testament clergy, the bishops, priests, and deacons, and what the service is that they offer to the Church.

All rights reserved. This book or any portion thereof may not be reproduced or used in any manner whatsoever without the express written permission of the publisher except for the use of brief quotations in a book review.

Translated from the original "О Священнослужителях" by Nikea Press, Copyright © Trading house «NIKEA», www.Nikeabooks.ru

ISBN: 978-1-950067-12-1 (Paperback)

Edited by Cynthia Hogg

First printing edition 2019

Exaltation Press
Grand Rapids, MI

www.ExaltationPress.com

For bulk orders, please contact editor@exaltationpress.com.

Table of Contents

THE TEMPLE 4
A LIFELONG SERVICE 6
A BELOVED PLACE 8
THE TEMPLE IN JERUSALEM 10
THE LAW 12
THE SON OF GOD 14
THE GREAT SACRIFICE 16
THE APOSTLES 18
DEACONS 20
BISHOPS 22
PRIESTS 24
THE LAYING-ON OF HANDS OF THE APOSTLES.......................................26
CONFESSION AND SPIRITUAL GUIDANCE 28
INTERESTING FACTS 30
WORKING TOGETHER 32

THE TEMPLE

The Church Temple is an amazing place where time and eternity are joined together. When we enter the Temple, we are Christ's guests. We speak to Him through the words of the prayers, through our actions, and through our thoughts. We listen to Him. Here, we become His disciples and friends through Communion in His Body and Blood. This might sound a little unusual.

But in the Temple, everything looks a little unusual. Of course, if your parents have brought you to Church since you were a baby then perhaps nothing in the Temple surprises you. People, whether they're little or grown up, can get used to anything. But just imagine that you've come to an Orthodox Temple for the first time and you'll be amazed by how this place is different from any other place, both inside and out.

The domes, the bells, the bright candles, the warm flickering of the lampadas that seem to make the faces of the saints come alive on the icons... The smell of the incense and the sound of the choir singing which makes your heart feel sad and joyful at the same time, but more importantly, makes your heart feel fresh, peaceful, and calm...

And then there are the people that look a little like the saints on the icons or even like wizards in their mysterious clothing. Their actions seem mysterious and in their hands they carry objects that look like they came out of the distant past. And just like the conductor of an orchestra, they direct the divine services, and bring our common prayer up to God.

5 The Clergy

A LIFELONG SERVICE

Who are they? Are they people? And if so, what kind of work are they doing?

Of course they're people. They're just like all other adults. But they've dedicated their whole lives to God in order to bring each person to Him, and to help and comfort everyone. To do that, they would have to love everyone like their own child, right? That's why we call these people "Father" and don't say "Michael works as a priest," because a job is something that you can change. Sometimes, for example, a person might work for awhile as a teacher and decide that he doesn't like it and go back to school and become a doctor. And if he doesn't like that, he can keep trying different jobs. But a priest, a Father, is something that you become once and remain for your whole life.

Only a man who takes it seriously can become a priest. Before such an important step, a man must prepare himself, pray, assist in the altar, study, and even take exams, because a priest helps people by treating their souls. That's more important even than treating their bodies. More than that, the clergy teach us about God. If, while teaching about God, a priest himself doesn't follow His commandments, teaching others to love and loving others himself, nothing good can come of his service. He would be like a drunk man telling others to be sober.

The Clergy

Service

That is what we call a priest's way of life. He serves God and the people, a sacred service. That is why we say that the priesthood is a sacred calling.

A BELOVED PLACE

Today there are many Temples. For example, in Russia, there are over 30,000 and there are more than 2,000 in the United States. Once, however, there was only one Temple. In the *whole world*. And in order to get there, people had to travel great distances.

Imagine your favorite place. For example, maybe it's a river with a sandy beach where you have a summer cabin. All year long, you look forward to summer so that you can go back and jump and splash in the cool, fresh water. Now imagine that it's the only beach like that in the world. During the winter, you could go to a pool somewhere and you'd enjoy it but even the best pool can't compare with that sandy beach because it's the only one in the whole world. There's only one.

Or imagine a flower. It's the only real one, surrounded by thousands of artificial flowers. They're bigger and brighter. But you know which one is real right away because of its sweet smell and gentle petals. It's alive and real…

> "When the soul sees the Lord, how meek and humble He is, then the soul itself is completely humbled and wants nothing as much as the humility of Christ. However long the soul lives on the Earth, it will continue to desire and seek that incomprehensible humility, which is impossible to forget. O Lord, how greatly You love mankind!"
>
> *St. Silouan the Athonite*

In the ancient world, there were many "artificial" temples. The human soul always looks to encounter God and eternity. That's how our souls are created. Besides, not everything in this world is under our control and so we need to ask help from the One who created the world. Only not everyone knew how to ask...

THE TEMPLE IN JERUSALEM

Not everyone knew how to ask and so they started to invent different protectors for themselves, spirits and gods that they believed took care of everything in the spiritual world for mankind. Perhaps you know how easy it can be to imagine something and then start to think that it's real, like an imaginary friend. So, people began to bow down and worship these imaginary "protectors" and make idols of them, both big and small. They brought sacrifices to their idols and tried to pray to them. Before long, they even invented their own priests and thought that they had secret knowledge and understood best what the idols wanted and how to gain their favor.

But the True God did not want these sacrifices, these pagan priests, or these invented idols. And whether someone wept in front of an idol, crushed with grief, or laughed out of joy, or whispered the secret desires of their heart, nothing changed. The idols were silent. The people suffered and felt that everything needed to change but they didn't understand how to do that.

There was only one true Temple and many had never even heard of it. In other words, there was only one true Temple in which people could talk to the True God in prayer. That Temple was located in Jerusalem.

The Clergy

What is a pagan priest?

In the ancient world, they were the ones who offered sacrifices to the idols. They also were scholars who studied the stars, trying to discover the laws of creation. The common people and even the kings were afraid of losing their favor, believing that the favor of the gods depended on these pagan priests.

THE LAW

Jerusalem was not the largest or most well known city. It was surrounded by stronger cities with rich palaces for proud kings, with those very same fake "temples" where pagan priests worshipped idols with great pomp, engaging in divination and fortune telling.

There was nothing like that in Jerusalem. The Jewish people living there were very simple. The place of the Temple, however, wasn't chosen by chance, but by God Himself, who didn't need the pomp and arrogance of the pagan temples. In the Temple of Jerusalem, people talked to the God who hears us and fills our hearts with joy, who answers us both directly and through other people and through our hearts and thoughts.

In that Temple, there were also priests serving constantly, offering sacrifices to God. However, although there was an outward similarity between them and the pagan priests, there was actually a big difference between them. The pagan priests led the people astray since they themselves didn't have the truth. The priests at the Temple in Jerusalem, however, taught the people

> Throughout all of history, God has worked to convince people to follow the right path and to keep them from stumbling. Unfortunately, people were not always obedient and thankful. Over time, most peoples, except for the Israelites, forgot the true God. Although the Israelites did not always behave themselves as they should, they still preserved the memory of God and did not worship idols.

The Clergy

the Law, which was given directly by God who, like a loving Father, did not really need sacrifices (which are only a sign of humanity's love and thanksgiving). Rather, His desire for us was that we live in eternal happiness.

THE SON OF GOD

Although God gave humanity the rules of eternal life, very often people did not follow them. The world exists according to its own rules. Some of those rules are visible. If you touch fire, you will always burn your hand. Other rules are invisible. An evil action will always burn the soul, although you cannot feel it right away. Each time, however, the burn grows larger and over time, the soul becomes practically incapable of doing good. It grows dark, hardened, and charred and it is deprived of eternal life.

And so, to save us from perishing, two thousand years ago, God became Man and came into the world. That day is one of the most important days in the whole history of the world. It began a new era in history and we count the years starting from that day. The Divine Holy Spirit overshadowed a young woman, who out of all the girls in the world was the most full of goodness. Her name was Mary, and later, she would be called the Theotokos. In a miraculous manner, she gave birth to Jesus Christ, the Son of God.

The prophets had long foretold that it was here, to Jerusalem, that the Son of God would come. He would make a Great Sacrifice after which everything would be different. Even the Temple in Jerusalem wouldn't be needed anymore after His sacrifice because God would be with every person in every place. All would hear about Him, even those who at the time were serving idols.

The miraculous Nativity of Jesus Christ took place in a very humble way. He wasn't born in a royal palace or in luxury, but in a small cave. That night, angels sang in the Heavens and a new, never-before-seen star was shining in the sky. By following that star, certain wise men who studied the stars (who themselves were pagan priests like we talked about before) learned of the birth of the King of the world. They set out on a journey to worship the Christ Child and to bring Him gifts.

THE GREAT SACRIFICE

Jesus walked the earth, preaching, healing, and raising the dead. Everywhere He went, His closest disciples went with Him.

However, many of the teachers and even the priests, who taught the Jewish people faith, began to envy Him. "Look! Jesus and His uneducated disciples are going all over the place, teaching the people," they said to each other, "and all are following Him and not paying any more attention to us. How can this be? No one is more righteous than we are!" And so not only envy, but also evil thoughts, took root in the hearts of these men who had been teachers and guides.

People with hearts that were dark and charred with envy were unable to bear the light coming from Jesus. Their envy made them blind. They slandered Jesus and sentenced Him to death.

The night before His arrest, the Lord Jesus Christ, knowing that He would soon be seized, took bread in His hands, broke it, and gave it to His disciples, saying, "This is My Body, which is given up to suffering for you. Do this always in remembrance of Me!"

Then, He took a cup of wine and said, "This cup is the New Testament in My Blood, which is shed for you!" as He gave the cup to the disciples.

This was the first Liturgy. It is called the Mystical Supper.

Later, Jesus was killed. He was nailed to the Cross. At the moment of His crucifixion, the sun grew dim and the world was immersed in darkness. Nature itself was unable to watch mankind mocking the One Who created the whole world. But Christ is the God-man and so death was unable to hold Him. In three days, He rose from the dead. The day of His resurrection changed the whole world. The way into the Kingdom of Heaven was opened to mankind. We gather for Liturgy every Sunday because Sunday is the Day of Resurrection.

At the moment of Christ's death, cracks appeared in the walls of the Temple of Jerusalem and the curtains were torn in two. It was as if God was showing that the time for this Temple had now passed. The Great Sacrifice was being accomplished, the sacrifice for which all of the Temple prayers, sacrifices, and services had been preparing.

THE APOSTLES

For forty days after His resurrection from the dead, the Lord Jesus Christ stayed with His disciples, telling them about love, service, and eternity. Then, Christ the God-Man ascended into Heaven to His Father, to join Heaven and Earth, God and mankind. However, He needed there to be people who could govern His Church here on earth.

Soon, the Holy Spirit descended on His disciples. It was incredible! There was a great noise in the sky above Jerusalem, as if there were a tornado or hurricane over the whole city. A fiery light shone above the disciples and they felt divine power. Their fear left them, their doubts vanished, and they were filled with confidence. Now, the disciples truly became Apostles. "Apostle" means someone sent by God. God sent them to establish our Church.

The hand of God invisibly worked through the hands of the Apostles and so they became the leaders of the Church, new grace-filled clergy who baptized and served Liturgy.

For two thousand years now, through a divine miracle, the bread and wine that are brought to Liturgy become the Body and Blood of Jesus Christ. While the Holy Gifts continue to look like bread and wine, when we taste them, we are united to the Risen Christ and He enters our hearts.

The Clergy

The day that the Holy Spirit descended, the Church was born. What is the Church? The Church is you and those in your parish, it is all Christians who have already entered eternity and all those still living here, both nearby and in faraway countries and, of course, it is Christ Himself, who always abides with us. People enter the Church through Holy Baptism and are joined with Christ during Liturgy.

DEACONS

After the descent of the Holy Spirit, when the Apostles preached, they baptized thousands of people who came from different places. Some of them had been pagans, others had been Jews. Their appearances were different. Some of them brought their great wealth to the Church while there were some others who came without even bread to eat. Imagine how difficult it must be to lead a group of people with such different desires and needs and to provide for all of them! And now imagine that there aren't just five or six people, but thousands!

And so the Apostles decided that they needed helpers. Otherwise, they wouldn't be able to build up the Church, since God had sent them to preach everywhere, even in distant countries. Their whole lives were now one continuous dangerous adventure. Angels went with them and the Lord Himself guided them. After the descent of the Holy Spirit, the Apostles were literally overflowing with Divine Grace. However, unlike the power-hungry pagan priests, who tried to keep everything for themselves, the Apostles wanted to share their gift with their brothers in the faith. When they had chosen helpers, the Apostles prayed and laid their hands on their heads and the Holy Spirit came upon them.

These helpers, who were called "deacons," helped the Apostles and the rest of the people in the Church. The deacons made sure that each person was healthy, well fed, and clothed. They made sure that each person had a place to sleep. And during Baptism and the Liturgy, the deacons always helped the Apostles. The diaconate is the first step of the priesthood.

The Clergy

Orarion

Stikharion

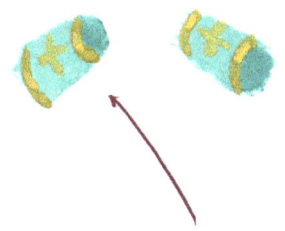

Cuffs (Epikmanikia)

Diaconal Vestments

The vestments that the clergy wear are symbolic. A symbol is when a visible object reminds us of something invisible, yet very important. The cuffs, or "epimanikia," that are worn by deacons, priests, and bishops symbolize their special service, since through their hands, the power of God works. The deacon's stole, or "orarion," symbolizes an angel's wings, since a deacon's service is like the service of the angels. And the stikharion, the robe that a deacon wears, shows the importance and majesty of the prayer of the Church.

BISHOPS

When the Apostles came to a particular city, they told the people about Christ. Then, they baptized them and gave them Communion before leaving to go preach in new places. Someone, however, needed to stay behind. And so, the Apostles chose bishops, usually one of the local people. They always tried to choose the best, men who were ready to give their whole life in service. The Apostles laid their hands on their heads and prayed to God with their whole hearts that the Holy Spirit would descend on these chosen men.

The service of the bishops was like the service of the Apostles themselves. The only difference was that the Apostles traveled from place to place while each bishop was the leader in a particular city, where he would preach, baptize, and serve Liturgy every Lord's day. Often, they had to do this secretly, in large houses that were hidden from the eyes of the world, in groves, in the catacombs, and in caves.

Pagan kings and priests, with all of their idols, were afraid that no one would need them anymore. The teachers in Jerusalem could not accept that now all people were equal before God and that the Temple of Jerusalem had lost its special status. Many persecuted the Church because they listened to other people's opinions, while others persecuted the Church because they were afraid of change and so they were unable to perceive the True God. Cowards and people who care too much about the opinions of others often choose the side of evil.

The Clergy

Episcopal Vestments

A mitre is a royal crown and a symbol of the glory of the future life. The omophorion is a symbol of Christ's love and mercy to all people. The sakkos is the part of a bishop's vestments that symbolizes the sufferings of Christ and the purple robe that the Roman soldiers mockingly dressed Him in before the Crucifixion. The panagia reminds us that our hearts should be full of love for Jesus Christ and His Mother, the All-holy Theotokos. A bishop's staff symbolizes his spiritual authority.

PRIESTS

As the people who were persecuting the Church saw their own failure, they grew more and more enraged. They threw Christians in prison, executed them, and threw them to wild beasts to be torn to pieces. They tried to force crowds of people to watch these tortures to scare them away from Christ. However, the firmness with which Christians faced their torments only convinced the people who witnessed their deaths to embrace the martyr's faith. God is not with pagan kings and priests but with Christians and so the Christians had nothing to fear.

More and more people came to the Church. Bishops were no longer able to take care of all the people alone. Often, the persecutors would first kill the bishop so that the Christian community in that city would lose its father and guide.

Then, the bishops decided that, together with God's people, they would choose people to serve with them, concelebrants, who themselves would be able to baptize, serve Liturgy, and lead the communities of Christians, or parishes, which were multiplying in every city. Often, they would choose one of the deacons, since they were experienced and had already dedicated their lives to service. God gave the bishops apostolic authority to lay their hands on His people to call down Divine Grace on them and to give them power, so that the Holy Spirit would overshadow them, fill what was lacking in them, and give them wisdom and understanding. Thus they became not just servants, but celebrants of the Mysteries.

That is how presbyters (or as we often call them, priests, or fathers) became part of the life of the Church.

25 The Clergy

Phelonion
Belt (Zone)
Cuffs (Epikmanikia)
Nabedrennik
Epitrachelion
Priest's Stikharion

Priestly Vestments

The snow-white stikarion is a sign of the spiritual purity and holiness to which God calls all of us. The zone, or "belt," is a symbol of a priest's readiness to serve the people. The epitrachelion, or "priestly stole," is a sign of how Divine power works through the service of the bishops and the priests. The pectoral cross reminds us that the love of Jesus Christ should live in the priest's heart. The priest's phelonion is a symbol of the sufferings of Christ and of the robe that the Roman soldiers mockingly put on Him before the Crucifixion.

THE LAYING-ON OF HANDS OF THE APOSTLES

After awhile, the persecution of the Church came to an end. The Temple of Jerusalem was gone, no one believed the pagan priests anymore, and even the kings and emperors learned more about Jesus Christ and His teachings and themselves became Christians. People began to build Christian Temples everywhere to serve Liturgy. And it was the presbyters, or as we often call them the priests, who were closest to the people and began to be called "Father." They are always near us. We see them every Sunday, hear their homilies, and turn to them for advice. We go to them for Confession and receive the Body and Blood of Christ from their hands.

> Ordination happens in order. First, someone is ordained a deacon and only then can he become a priest. And if someone is chosen to be a bishop, he must first be a priest. In order to consecrate a bishop, the bishops of neighboring cities gather. There must be at least two of them but usually there are more.

There is also a bishop of your city. He serves in the main Church of your diocese, called the Cathedral. Just like the Apostles, the bishop prays and lays his hands on the heads of those that he chooses, ordaining them as deacons and priests, and God, just like before, overshadows them with grace and the power to serve us.

Of course, there is no one who never makes mistakes, gets tired, or sins. Priests are people and so all of that happens with them, too. The grace that they are given in ordination doesn't make someone wise or a saint. It strengthens him so that he himself can strive for holiness and wisdom. If he is openhearted to everyone and keeps his heart with God, then all will go well.

The apostolic laying-on of hands has been going on uninterrupted in the Church for two thousand years. It is like a pure river, where the water is the grace of the Holy Spirit. From generation to generation, we take that water and drink and are joined with the river's source - God Himself. His divine hand works through the hands of the bishops. Through ordination, that thread of service to the Church of Christ stretches from the days of the Apostles to our own days. The priest in your parish is connected in that way to the Apostles and has their blessing on his service.

Ranks of Bishops

Bishops who administer large dioceses carry the important title of "metropolitan" or "archbhishop." The head bishop of an entire Local Church often has the title of "patriarch." A patriarch is a father of fathers, a father to the bishops and priests. There are fifteen of these local Churches around the world. They are friendly to each other and together comprise Orthodoxy, or the Orthodox Church, the head of which is the Lord Jesus Christ Himself.

CONFESSION AND SPIRITUAL GUIDANCE

Like it or not, all of us sin. Often. God is always ready to forgive us, no matter how serious our mistakes, as long as we have in our heart the desire to correct our mistakes. However, we don't always have the strength to correct ourselves. Sometimes, our bad habits get mixed in with our desires.

Christ Himself, through His apostles, the clergy, and all Christians, has established His Church in such a way that everything in it leads to Him. Bad actions, on the other hand, lead us away from God, which is why our soul feels heavy when we sin. When we sin, our soul gets heavy, as if it were turning from a bird that could fly freely to Heaven into a lifeless stone.

Confession is a true gift from God. It gives us wings. It gives us a way of receiving forgiveness and comfort. We tell God about our sins, our bad habits. We feel worried. God, however, not only forgives us but also gives us strength to struggle against and overcome those sins. Here again, much depends on the person. If we are sincere in our desire to correct ourselves,

> **A Spiritual Father**
>
> As you grow up, you'll need to find yourself a guide – a priest who understands you better than others and who you trust to open up to and whose advice you value. There are many priests, but you will have only one guide. That guide is called a "spiritual father."

then God's strength enters our souls. The priest hears our Confession but it is God Himself who receives it.

Usually, we begin to go to Confession when we turn seven or perhaps a little later. The most important thing is that there be a real desire for Confession. And that the desire is yours.

INTERESTING FACTS

Klobuk

Mantiya

Only a monastic priest can become a bishop. In other words, only someone who has renounced everything of his own. It wasn't always like that. Many of the first bishops were family men. However, it quickly became clear that this service made it impossible for the bishop to care for his wife and children. So that no one would suffer from having an absent father, the Church began to ordain only monks as bishops.

Sometimes, monks also become deacons or priests. Monks are Christians who make a conscious choice to renounce money and possessions and who decide not to marry. Their whole lives are dedicated to prayer and service. Usually, monks live and work together in monasteries. There are monasteries for men and monasteries for women. There's even a monastic state, the peninsula of Mt. Athos in Greece. It is a special place. People call it the Holy Mountain and the Theotokos herself cares for it.

Married men are also ordained priests and deacons. Some of them, after their ordination, take off their wedding rings as a sign that from now on, they belong not only to their families but also to the Church of Christ and all the people in it.

Many of the vestments that clergy wear have a royal origin and were given to them by kings and emperors. That happened after the persecution stopped and Christians were no longer being killed. Now, even the pagan emperors began to believe in God and were baptized and became humble people. They were ashamed of what their predecessors had done and they wanted to show all the people that the service that the clergy were offering was just as important as the service kings showed their people and even greater and so they asked the clergy to accept some pieces of royal clothing.

WORKING TOGETHER

Priests have many responsibilities. You may have noticed that yourself. Often, they're so busy that it's hard for them to find time to be with their families. But in the Christian Church, we all serve together. We are all children of God and all equal before Him. Even Liturgy is something that we all participate in. It's wrong for us to think that we should only come to Church in time for the service and then hurry back to our daily lives. The Church is all of us and so each of us who is in the Church should look for our way to serve. Some people help the priest in the altar, others sing, others write articles and books, while still others care for children, visit the sick and elderly, or gather funds to help the poor. There's no end to the ways we can serve. We can all serve the Church together. Isn't that interesting? Think about it... What would you like to do?

www.ingramcontent.com/pod-product-compliance
Lightning Source LLC
Chambersburg PA
CBHW051351110526
44591CB00025B/2965